OUR PLANET

Forests

DAVID LAMBERT

Troll Associates

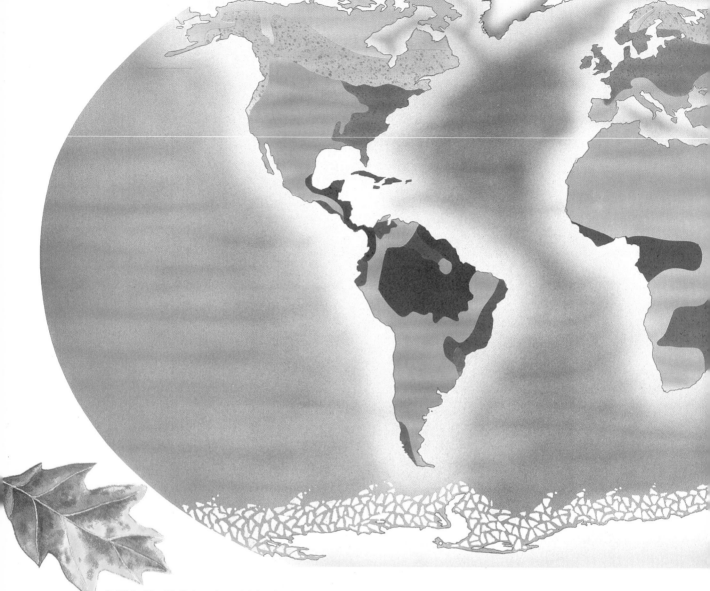

Published by Troll Associates, Mahwah, New Jersey 07430

Design by James Marks, London.

Picture research by Jan Croot.

Illustrators: Martin Camm: pages 16-17, 20-21, 26, 28, 29; Chris Forsey: pages 4-5; David More: pages 6-7, 23; Mike Roffe: pages 24-25; Paul Sullivan: pages 22-23; Ian Thompson: pages 2-3; Phil Weare: pages 10-11, 13, 18-19; David Webb: pages 7, 8, 11, 14.

Printed in the U.S.A.

10 9 8 7 6 5 4 3 2 1

Library of Congress Cataloging-in-Publication Data

Lambert, David, (date)
    Forests / by David Lambert; illustrated by Martin Camm . . . [et al.].
        p.   cm.—(Our planet)
    Summary: Describes the formation, characteristics, and plant and animal life of different types of forests.
    ISBN 0-8167-1971-3 (lib. bdg.)   ISBN 0-8167-1972-1 (pbk.)
    1. Forest ecology—Juvenile literature. [1. Forests and forestry. 2. Forest ecology. 3. Ecology.] I. Camm, Martin, ill. II. Title. III. Series.
QH541.5.F6L36   1990
574.5'2642—dc20   89-20311

Taiga (needle-leaved forests)

Temperate deciduous forests

Tropical rain forests

Tropical deciduous forests

Map: Major forests of the world

Title page:
Beech trees in spring

CONTENTS

Forests Past and Present

Millions of years ago, this is how a forest would have looked. Even today the earliest forests are useful to us. They now lie crushed and buried deep underground, but we dig mines to get coal from them. When you turn on a light, the electricity you use might come from coal-fired power stations.

Without forests, you would not be reading this book. Nor, probably, would you be sitting on your chair.

Even today, wood is used for buildings, boats, and furniture. Forest crops provide us with bananas, rubber, medicines, and much more.

Much of the oxygen we breathe escaped into the air from countless millions of forest leaves. Leaves also give off moisture, which helps produce the rain needed for crops to grow.

Forests are home to millions of plants and animals, and to some people. Different soils and climates have created a rich variety of forests, each with different kinds of wildlife and trees.

Forests like this existed when dinosaurs roamed the Earth. Over millions of years, rotting trees from these forests gradually turned into coal.

Temperate Forests

Forests grow wherever there is a long enough growing season and enough water. In mild climates, particularly in parts of North America, Europe, and China, temperate forests thrive.

Most of the trees you find in temperate forests are *deciduous*. This means they shed their leaves once a year. This helps them to survive the winter. Forests act like giant sponges, soaking up water from the ground and then releasing it into the air through their leaves. In the cold winter weather they cannot obtain enough water from the ground to replace what they release, so they shed their leaves. Without leaves, they are also better able to withstand strong winter winds. As the green fades from the dying leaves, their previously hidden reds and yellows seem to set the woods on fire.

Oak and birch

A walk through a temperate forest might take you underneath a "roof" of tall broadleaved trees, such as beeches, chestnuts and oaks. Above you rise smaller broadleaved trees, perhaps birches or maples. Beneath these stand hawthorns, dogwoods, evergreens such as holly, and other shrubby trees and bushes. In spring, the forest floor gleams with celandines, primroses, bluebells, and other flowers. All grow in soil made rich by rotted leaves.

6

↑ Fall colors reflected in a lake. The reds and yellows are there throughout the year, but only show when green fades from the leaves in the fall.

Beech leaves and flowers

Oak leaves in the fall

Needle-Leaved Forests

The Siberian Forest, in Russia, is larger than the United States. Yet this vast sprawling wilderness forms only part of the *taiga*, the largest forest on earth. The taiga crosses the northern parts of three continents – North America, Europe and Asia – like a great green belt wrapped around the world.

Northern forests have harsh climates. Winters are long, and so cold that tree trunks sometimes split with a bang as their sap turns to ice.

Larch

Only the hardiest trees can endure such cold. Among them are firs, pines, spruces, and larches. All are *conifers*, trees that bear their seeds in cones. With their sloping sides and springy branches, conifers can bend in fierce winds or under snow. Most stay evergreen, since their needle-shaped leaves are tough enough to resist freezing.

North America has some interesting conifers. The giant sequoias of California are the world's largest living things, and the gnarled little bristlecone pines are the oldest. Tallest of all trees are the coast redwoods that grow in foggy parts of Oregon and California.

Douglas fir

Mixed forests, which include both broadleaved and needle-leaved trees, are common in many parts of the world.

→ Conifer branches bend under snow, instead of breaking.

Tropical Rain Forests

Tropical rain forests grow on moist warm lowlands near the equator. The largest are found in South America's Amazon Valley and in central Africa.

From the air the *canopy*, or "roof," of a rain forest looks like a sea of rounded treetops. Here and there, a giant tree towers above the rest, like a massive umbrella. If you dropped from a helicopter and climbed down

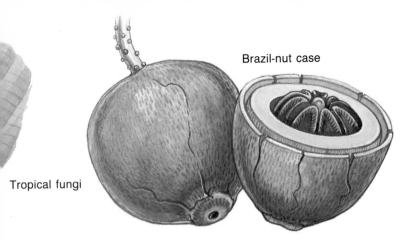

Brazil-nut case

Tropical fungi

← Colorful fungi (left) sprout from rotted leaves and fallen branches on the floor of South American rain forests.

Brazil nuts (right) grow in the forests of South America. They have hard, woody cases, which parrots and macaws crack open, using their sharp beaks.

through the canopy, you would find a layer of shorter trees soaking up soft light from above. Lower still, you would come to palms, tiny trees, and shrubs. Below that, on the forest floor, fungi sprout from dead leaves and fallen branches. Down here, it is so dark that few other plants can survive.

In forests like this, trees grow fast and in great variety. During a five-minute walk, you might spot 200 different kinds, 20 times as many as in a North American forest. Many have broad leaves with a long pointed tip, so the rain runs off. Most are evergreen, shedding just a few leaves at a time. All year you would find some in flower or laden with fruit.

← A giant rain-forest tree has *buttress roots* jutting out from the trunk to support it. A crown of leafy branches, as big as a soccer field, spreads out from the top of the tall bare trunk.

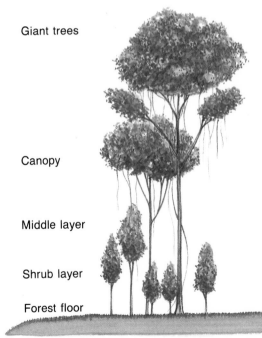

Giant trees

Canopy

Middle layer

Shrub layer

Forest floor

11

Plants on Other Plants

In their bid to reach light, some rain-forest plants grow piggyback on others.

Lianas are woody climbers, like ivy but much larger. They start life as tiny trees sprouting from the forest floor. Soon they hook onto large tree trunks and climb high into the canopy. Giant lianas have stems as thick as a man's thigh, strung in rope-like loops from tree to tree. They can be over 1,000 feet long.

If you climbed a tall rain-forest tree, you would discover hundreds of different plants sprouting from its branches. Plants that use trees for support, in order to reach the light, are called *epiphytes*. Some, like Spanish moss, are *airplants*, which get most of the nourishment that they need from the air. Plants which we grow indoors as houseplants, such as orchids, ferns, and bromeliads, sprout from the trees' branches. They root in rotting leaves in cracks in the bark. A bromeliad's leaves act like drainpipes to funnel water down into the plant. A large one can hold as much as a bucket of water.

Not all plants are harmless to those they grow on. Some, like the strangler fig, kill their host tree. A plant that grows at the expense of another is called a *parasite*.

↑ Bromeliads and orchids growing on a rain-forest tree.

↓ Stinking-corpse lily. This rain-forest plant has the largest flowers on Earth.

← A twisting liana in the Amazon rain forest, in South America.

13

Seasonal Tropical Forests

Many hot countries have long dry spells between the rainy seasons. Unlike the trees of the rain forests, which have a plentiful supply of water, trees that grow in dry areas have to preserve moisture.

Burma's forests are famous for their teak trees, and for the elephants trained to shift the huge teak logs. As the dry season starts, teak trees shed their leaves to save moisture. Fires sometimes start in the dry months, but the trees' thick bark resists burning. When the rains arrive, the teak trees put out new leaves. In rich soil, teak can grow very fast. In only 15 years, a seedling can develop into a tree more than 60 feet tall.

Baobab tree

The banyan tree of India starts life growing on another tree. As it grows, it sends roots down to the ground. Eventually these form into tree trunks, and the host tree is killed. One banyan tree in India has transformed itself into a forest of 3,000 trees.

In northeast Brazil and parts of Africa, much drier seasonal forests exist. *Dry forests* tend to have short trees with flat tops, which provide welcome shade for animals. Their bark is thick and they produce small leaves in the wet season.

↑ Elephants can pick up heavy teak logs with their trunks. It takes years to train them, but they move through the forest more easily than machines.

← Dry forests often have short, flat-topped trees, like this acacia.

In some dry forests, the leaves are nothing more than spines or thorns. Certain dry-forest trees have developed bottle-shaped trunks in which they store water. A giant African baobab tree may hold enough to fill 700 barrels. During the long dry season the baobab remains leafless to reduce water loss. It provides welcome shelter for many animals of the African grasslands.

↑ This mangrove tree beside the Indian Ocean has *prop roots* curving down from its trunk.

→ Gorillas are the largest living apes. They are found in the mountain forests of Central Africa.

Mangrove and Mountain Forests

Mangrove forests grow along warm muddy seashores beside the Pacific, Atlantic, and Indian Oceans. Ordinary trees cannot grow in salty water, but mangroves can. Their shiny leaves give off unwanted salt for the rain to wash away. Most trees cannot grow in suffocating mud, but mangroves thrive there. Some push up lots of roots that poke out of the mud like little periscopes. Many send out prop roots that curve down from the trunks and branches. All these roots above ground take in air for the main roots buried in the mud.

Giant pandas feed mainly on certain kinds of bamboo and are also fond of honey. They live in the mountain forests of northern China.

Mangrove forests even invade the sea. Their long pointed seeds drop from the branches into the mud below. There they form new trees. Mud becomes lodged around the roots until it forms new land for more trees to grow on.

Tropical mountains also have their own kind of forests. On the lower slopes of some African and Asian mountains, forests of bamboo, a giant woody grass, grow as tall as a church steeple. Higher up, in the moist, foggy mountain air, grow damp, dripping cloud forests. Here the trees are hung with moss and ferns, which also cover the ground like a shaggy carpet.

Life Among the Trees

All seems hushed and still as you step inside a tropical rain forest. Yet forests teem with hidden animals. Most of the world's 30 million different creatures are forest dwellers. In the rain forests of South America you find the world's largest spider, the tarantula. One type even preys on small birds. Here, too, is the heaviest snake, the anaconda, which coils itself around its victims until they can no longer breathe.

Above your head, other creatures cling, climb, leap, or fly. Sleepy-looking sloths and porcupines clamber slowly up trunks. Tree snakes and tree lizards are excellent climbers. Frogs with sticky toe pads leap from leaf to leaf.

The finest acrobats of the forest are the monkeys and squirrels.

Woolly monkey

Flying squirrel

Fruit bat

Flying lizard

Sometimes they drop the height of a
four-story building before landing safely
on a branch. No less daring are the
flying lizards and snakes. These do not
really fly, but glide from tree to tree.
The lizards use webs of skin as parachutes, and
the snakes flatten their bodies to break their fall.
But the true forest fliers are the bats and brightly
colored butterflies and birds.

Some creatures never leave the leafy roof of the
rain forest. Until people began exploring the
treetops in the 1970s, many of these animals had
never been seen by man.

Eaters and Eaten

Every forest has its own *food chain*. The plants make food from chemicals and water in soil and air. And the animals eat the plants, or one another.

In a South American rain forest, trees supply food for many creatures. Sloths and howler monkeys munch the leaves. Tiny hummingbirds hover near the flowers, sucking the nectar through tube-shaped tongues. Toucans have long beaks to pluck fruit from twigs too slender to stand on, and macaws' beaks are strong enough to crack the woody cases of Brazil nuts.

The capybara lives on river banks in the Amazon rain forest. Its name means "rat as big as a pig."

The trees also provide useful cover for hunters. Jaguars and huge snakes suddenly attack ground animals such as the capybara, the world's largest rodent. Sometimes a harpy eagle swoops down and snatches an unsuspecting monkey or sloth from a branch.

Overhead, turkey vultures circle patiently. A keen sense of smell enables them to find a dead animal hidden from view on the ground below.

Rotting leaves and animal corpses and droppings nourish fungi, insects, and microbes living on the forest floor. These break down plant and animal remains into chemicals that nourish plants. Plants then become food for animals — and so the chain continues.

Two-toed sloth

20

↑ Jaguars are good climbers and patient hunters. They lie hidden in the branches, then suddenly spring down on animals on the forest floor.

Porcupine

↑ Young Amerindian boys are skillful hunters. They learn how to use a bow and arrow and a blowpipe at an early age.

→ Amerindians use dugout canoes for hunting and fishing. Canoes are a useful way of traveling through the dense Amazon forest.

People of the Forests

Natives of tropical rain forests developed special skills to help them survive. They do not use the machines and products most of us rely on. Whether they are Amerindians in South America, Pygmies in Africa, or Dayaks in Borneo, they know which plants and animals are safe to eat. Scientists are only now discovering medicines from rain-forest plants that have long been used by forest dwellers.

The rain forest provides Amerindians with everything they need. They live in huts made with a framework of poles and a thatched roof. Their canoes are hollowed tree trunks. Their razors are sharp grass blades, and they even sew with needles made from the tips of hard, pointed leaves.

The fleshy cassava root is poisonous, yet Amerindians make bread from it after taking out the poison. They use blowpipes to kill monkeys, firing darts dipped in a deadly plant poison called curare. Other plant poisons are put into rivers to stun fish, which the Amerindians scoop up in nets woven from plant fibers. These skills are now disappearing as forest people take up modern ways of life.

The seeds of the annatto tree provide Amerindians with orange dye, which they use as body paint. Other people use the dye to color fabrics, varnishes, and foods such as butter and cheese.

23

Cropping Forests

Just as farmers grow wheat, foresters grow and harvest crops of trees. After harvesting, trees often sprout again naturally. But foresters also create manmade forests. With a single tree-planting machine, two people can plant 10,000 seedlings a day. More than a billion trees are planted each year in the United States alone.

A few years after planting, foresters thin out the young trees so those left will grow more strongly. They also remove diseased or weak trees, feed the soil, and spray the trees with chemicals to protect them against insects and disease. Broad strips are cut through forests to prevent fires from spreading. When fires start, water bombs are dropped from firefighting planes to try to put the fires out.

Conifers, or "softwood trees," are the foresters' favorite crop, because they grow faster than broadleaved, or "hardwood," trees. After about 40 years, they are ready for felling. Machines are used to cut the trees down and chop them into logs. These are then carried by trucks or floated down rivers to sawmills for slicing into planks, or to papermills for pulping.

Timber for building and papermaking comes mainly from northern softwood forests. Furniture is mostly made from hardwood trees grown in temperate regions or the tropics. Surprisingly, even today more wood is used for heating and cooking than for any other purpose.

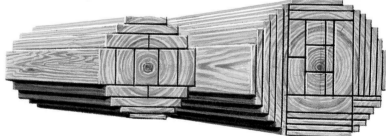

← At a sawmill, logs are cut according to their size and the type of wood. Computerized scanners decide which sort of cut will waste the least wood. The best timber comes from the part surrounding the core. Waste pieces go into the chipper. The chips are then used to make paper.

↑ Shifting logs outside a South American sawmill. Tractors, cranes, and forklift trucks are used to lift timber onto the mill's conveyor belts.

25

Vanishing Forests

A third of the Earth's land surface is covered by forest. But every year, vast areas of forest are felled for timber or burned to clear land for crops or cattle. In two hours, a team of foresters using felling machines can cut down 1,000 tons of trees.

Within your lifetime, the world's tropical rain forests could vanish, perhaps forever. Forest people would then lose their homes. Timber and firewood would become scarcer. Wild plants useful as foods or medicines would disappear, and thousands of animal species would die out.

Land cleared of tropical rain forest soon becomes useless. Rain washes away the loose soil until only scraggly bushes will grow there. Then rainwater pours down the bare hillsides, flooding the ground below and filling rivers with mud.

Worse still, burning forests give off carbon dioxide, which traps extra heat in the atmosphere. This adds to what is known as the *greenhouse effect*, which is warming the Earth's atmosphere and could eventually even melt part of the polar ice sheets.

The golden-lion tamarin monkey **(above)** and the powerful harpy eagle **(below)** live in the forests of Central and South America. Both could die out if more forests are destroyed.

→ A dropped match can start a forest fire that spreads 10 miles in just one hour.

26

Saving the Forests

One day in 1973, woodcutters came to fell trees in an Indian village. The villagers objected, and clasped the trees until the woodcutters went away without felling them. Tree-hugging gradually spread through India. As a result, many forest trees have been saved.

More recently, scientists and the people of Tasmania stopped the building of a dam that would have drowned one of the last truly wild temperate forests in the world.

Even lost forests may be replaced. South Korea has covered bare mountainsides with pines, and China has planted lands as big as Arizona with forests.

Timber merchants know it makes sense to plant young trees when they cut down old ones. Near Brazil's Jari River, a rain forest twice as large as Delaware is being cleared and replanted

Many beautiful animals, such as the blue macaw **(left)** and the indri **(above)**, will only survive if their forest homes are saved.

with a few fast-growing kinds of trees. But this will not put back the rich variety of trees and wildlife that has been lost.

Only leaving large stretches of forest untouched or removing trees a few at a time keeps forests unharmed. Forestry methods of this kind were first used in North America. Now many countries have national forests where visitors can see animals living in the wild and enjoy the natural beauty of trees.

← National parks make a safe home for endangered animals such as the North American black bear. Black bears still live in the Olympic Rain Forest in the state of Washington. This is the last rain forest left in North America, and has been a national park since 1938.

↑ Orang-utans, like this young one, live in Malaysia. Their name means ''man of the forest.'' Many of the forests where they used to live have been cut down for timber.

→ The koala eats only six kinds of eucalyptus leaf. Its food trees were rapidly disappearing, but now more have been planted and the number of koalas is steadily increasing.

Fact File

Ancient Forests

The first forests appeared about 360 million years ago. Fragments of trees which are millions of years old have been preserved in rocks. In Arizona's famous Petrified Forest, you can see ancient tree trunks that have turned to stone. Remains of plants or animals that have hardened into rock or stone are called *fossils*.

Where Forests Grow

Forests are able to grow where there is more than 8 inches of rain a year and at least three months of the year are free from frost. Rain forests in the tropics have an average rainfall of 60 to 100 inches a year.

Variety of Trees

Nearly 1,200 *species*, or kinds, of tree grow in the U.S. In just one tropical rain forest, there can be as many as 3,000 species of trees and shrubs.

Tallest Tree

One coast redwood in California is 370 feet tall. A eucalyptus in Australia measured in 1872 was 435 feet tall.

Largest Tree

A giant sequoia in California named the "General Sherman" weighs 2,500 tons. It is thought to be 2,500 years old.

Fastest-Growing Tree

An acacia tree in Malaysia is reported to have grown 35 feet in 13 months.

↑ *Petrified tree trunks*　　　　↓ *Giant sequoia*

Oldest Living Tree

The oldest living tree is a bristlecone pine in California known as "Methuselah," which is 4,600 years old.

Oldest Surviving Species

The Chinese ginkgo, or maidenhair tree, first appeared at least 160 million years ago.

Heaviest Wood

Black ironwood from Africa is so heavy that it sinks in water. 1 cubic foot weighs nearly 94 lbs.

Lightest Wood

The wood of the *Aeschynomene hispida* tree in Cuba is 34 times lighter than black ironwood. 1 cubic foot weighs 2.8 lbs.

The lightest wood commonly available is balsa, though its weight can vary.

Forests of the World

Some continents have larger areas of forest than others. Forest covers:

    57% of Southeast Asia
    54% of South America
    32% of North and Central
      America
    32% of Europe
    32% of North, Central and
      East Asia
    24% of Africa
    18% of Australasia
    13% of South Asia

Altogether, forest covers 30% of the Earth's land surface.

↓ *Bristlecone pine*

Vanishing Forests

Tropical rain forests once covered nearly one tenth of the Earth's surface. Each year, an area about as big as Oregon is destroyed. About 100 acres of rain forest vanish every minute.

In Central America, two-thirds of the forests have been felled to provide land for cattle.

More than half the trees in Germany, Switzerland, and Holland have died because of acid rain.

Forest Fires

Every year there are about 100,000 forest fires in the U.S.

A satellite passing over the Amazon rain forest in South America once spotted 8,000 large fires in just one day.

Riches of the Rain Forest

One in four of the items stocked by an ordinary drugstore (such as medicines and cosmetics) contains some ingredient that comes from rain-forest plants.

It is estimated that half of the Earth's plant and animal species are found in tropical rain forests.

How Wood is Used

Each year the world uses more than 4 billion cubic yards of wood. About 54% of all the wood used is burned, mainly for heating and cooking. About 46% is made into building materials, furniture, paper, and other products.

31

Index

Picture Credits
Heather Angel: pages 1, 31
Hutchison Library: John Hatt 10-11;
Bernard Régent 14-15;
Jesco von Püttkamer 22-23
South American Pictures: 12, 16-17,
20-21, 24-25, 30 (top)
Survival Anglia: Jeff Foott 26-27;
Dieter & Mary Plage 28-29
Zefa (UK) Ltd: 6-7, 8-9, 30 (bottom)